BRAIN GAMES

MW01132524

KITCHEN SCIENCE EXPERIMENTS

pil

Publications International, Ltd.

Written by Nicole Sulgit and Beth Taylor with additional material from Adam Parrilli
Photo styling by Nick LaShure, Ashley Joyce, and Nicole Sulgit
Photography by Christopher Hiltz, Nick LaShure and Nicole Sulgit
Additional images from Shutterstock.com

ISBN: 978-1-64558-522-0

Manufactured in China.

8 7 6 5 4 3 2 1

SAFETY WARNING
All of the experiments and activities in this book MUST be performed with adult supervision. All projects contain a degree of risk, so carefully read all instructions before you begin and make sure that you have safety materials such as goggles, gloves, etc. Also make sure that you have safety equipment, such as a fire extinguisher and first aid kit, on hand. You are assuming the risk of any injury by conducting these activities and experiments. Publications International, Ltd. will not be liable for any injury or property damage.

Let's get social!
@Publications_International
@PublicationsInternational
@BrainGames.TM
www.pilbooks.com

CONTENTS

28

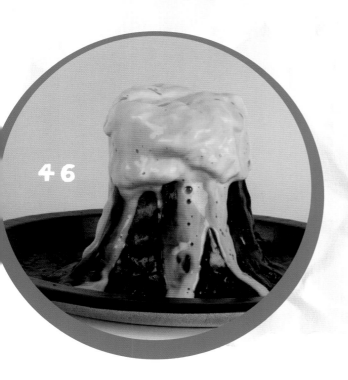

46

What do a rock, a river, and a raccoon have in common?

They are all made up of matter. Chemistry is the science that studies matter. What are substances made of? What are their properties? How do they interact with each other? How do they change?

ATOMS

One of the smallest building blocks of the universe is called the atom. Atoms are made up of positive particles called protons, negative particles called electrons, and neutral particles called neutrons. When an atom has the same number of protons and electrons, it is neutral. But atoms can gain or lose electrons. They are called ions when this happens.

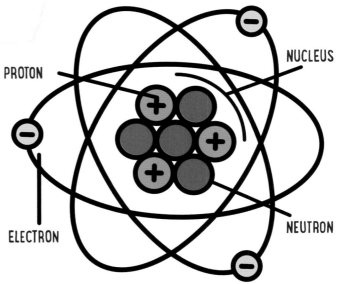

PROTON

NUCLEUS

ELECTRON

NEUTRON

WATER MOLECULE

ELEMENTS

An element is a substance made up of a single type of atom. Gold, oxygen, and helium are all elements. Elements join together to form compounds. Water contains the elements of oxygen and hydrogen, for example.

HOW MANY ATOMS MAKE UP THE HUMAN BODY?

Billions and billions. In fact, **7,000,000,000,000,000,000,000,000,000**. The human body is mostly made up of the elements oxygen, carbon, hydrogen, nitrogen, calcium, and phosphorous. There are some other elements too, like sodium.

MASS

Mass is how much matter an object contains. Sometimes, a big object can have very little mass. A big sheet of paper could have less mass than a small rock. Mass is not exactly the same as weight. Weight is the force applied to the object by gravity. Your mass stays the same wherever you are in the universe, but your weight changes in places with more or less gravity. Someone who weighs 75 pounds on Earth would weigh about 175 pounds on Jupiter, but only about 5 pounds on Pluto!

STATES OF MATTER

The same matter can exist in different states. For example, the compound H_2O, two hydrogen atoms combined with one oxygen atom, can exist as a solid in the form of ice, a liquid in the form of water, and a gas in the form of water vapor.

SOLID   LIQUID   GAS

In a solid state, molecules are tightly packed together. In a gas, they float more freely.

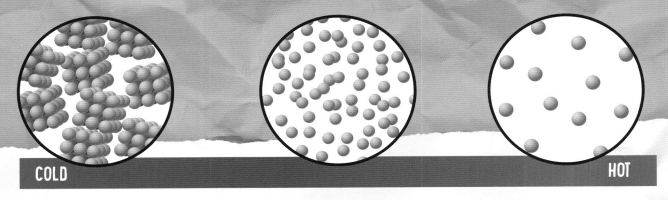

COLD   HOT

FROM STATE TO STATE

Temperature affects state. Each substance has a melting point where a solid becomes liquid and a freezing point where a liquid becomes solid. Many metals have a very high melting point. The melting point of gold, for example, is very high. That's why a gold necklace doesn't just melt in a puddle when it sits in a jewelry box. It needs to reach 1,948 degrees Fahrenheit or 1,064 degrees Celsius. Other metals, like Caesium, melt just above room temperature.

When a substance changes from gas to liquid, the process is called condensation. When a substance changes from liquid to gas, it is called vaporization.

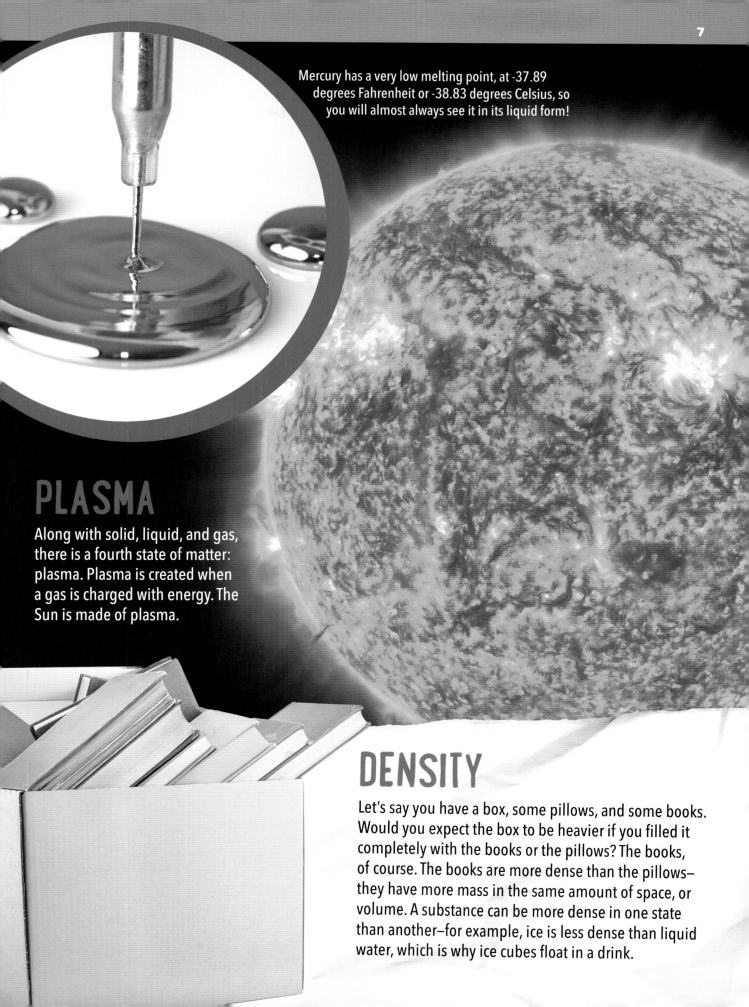

Mercury has a very low melting point, at -37.89 degrees Fahrenheit or -38.83 degrees Celsius, so you will almost always see it in its liquid form!

PLASMA

Along with solid, liquid, and gas, there is a fourth state of matter: plasma. Plasma is created when a gas is charged with energy. The Sun is made of plasma.

DENSITY

Let's say you have a box, some pillows, and some books. Would you expect the box to be heavier if you filled it completely with the books or the pillows? The books, of course. The books are more dense than the pillows—they have more mass in the same amount of space, or volume. A substance can be more dense in one state than another—for example, ice is less dense than liquid water, which is why ice cubes float in a drink.

SLIME

Make your own slime and see how it behaves differently from other liquids.

MATERIALS

- 1½–2 cups cornstarch
- 1 cup warm water
- ¼ cup shampoo
- Food coloring
- Wax paper
- Large mixing bowl
- Spatula
- Tablespoon

Step 1

Place wax paper on your work surface. Add 1½ cups of cornstarch to the mixing bowl. Dip your hands in the cornstarch. *What does the powder feel like?*

Step 2

Add ¼ cup shampoo to mixing bowl.

Step 3

Mix a few drops of food coloring into a cup of warm water. Stir well with a tablespoon.

Step 4

Add a few tablespoonfuls of colored water to the mixing bowl at a time. Keep stirring the water into the cornstarch with a spatula.

Step 5

Continue adding water a few tablespoonfuls at a time until the mixture turns into a thick paste. Add cornstarch if the mixture gets too runny; add water if it becomes too thick.

Step 6

Grab a handful of the slime and observe how it changes when you handle it different ways. *What happens when you roll it between your hands, squeeze it in your fist, press it onto a surface, or let it run through your fingers?*

HOW DOES IT WORK?

Slime isn't your typical liquid or solid. Applying pressure to the slime increases its viscosity, or thickness. When you handle the slime gently, the starch molecules can move around, suspended in the water. This makes a slow-flowing liquid.

But when you press down suddenly on the slime, the starch molecules lock together, making the slime feel more solid. Slime is an example of a non-Newtonian fluid. The viscosity of non-Newtonian fluids changes depending on the forces of pressure applied.

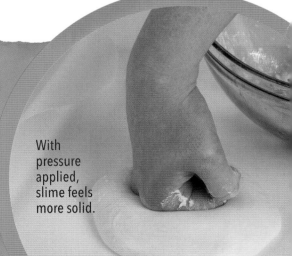

With pressure applied, slime feels more solid.

LIQUID LAYERS

Different liquids have different densities. Build a colorful tower by layering these liquids on top of each other.

MATERIALS

- Honey or maple syrup
- Water
- Vegetable or olive oil
- A measuring cup with a pouring spout
- A glass
- A variety of solid objects with different masses such as:
  - Berries
  - Grapes or cherry tomatoes
  - Coins
  - Marshmallows
  - Raisins or beans
- Food coloring (optional)

Step 1

Spoon or pour the honey or syrup into the bottom of a glass.

Step 2

If desired, add a few drops of food coloring to water. Slowly pour the water into the glass. You may want to tilt the glass at an angle for the best results.

Step 3

Because water is less dense than honey, it will settle on top of the honey.

Step 4

Pour the oil on top of the water.
A slow, careful pour will work best.

Step 5

Begin gently dropping objects into the glass. *Do they settle to the bottom? Rest in the middle layer? Float on top?*

Coins settle to the bottom.

A bean is not quite as dense—
it rests on top of the honey.

Blackberries are less dense than beans.

A marshmallow is very light!

Oil spills can be difficult to clean up. Oil spreads rapidly across the top of the water, presenting a danger to waterbirds and marine life. Wind and currents spread the spill out from its place of origin.

ZOOMING BEANS

Defy gravity to make a bean "dance" in water!

MATERIALS

- Two glasses
- Bottled or tap water
- Carbonated water or clear carbonated soda
- Pinto beans

step 1

Pour regular water into one glass, and a carbonated beverage into the other.

step 2

Drop a few beans into each glass of water. *What happens?*

HOW DOES IT WORK?

The beans go up and down in the carbonated water. The bubbles of carbonation attach to the surface of the bean and lift it up. As bubbles pop and new bubbles reform, the bean falls and rises.

This experiment works best with fresh soda with many bubbles. Raisins are a great alternative if you don't have beans.

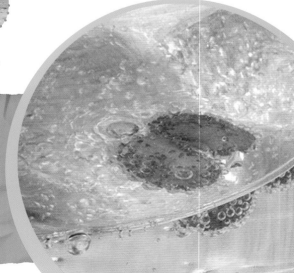

When you open a can of soda, you hear a sound. When cans are sealed at the factory, carbon dioxide is sealed in them. Opening the can releases the pressure and some of the carbon dioxide.

Over time, bottled soda or other carbonated beverages goes flat as the carbon dioxide slowly escapes.

People can buy products that add carbonation to water and even make their own soda at home.

THE GROWING MARSHMALLOW

Create a marshmallow monster in your microwave!

MATERIALS

- Marshmallows
- Food coloring
- Toothpicks
- Microwave-safe plate
- Microwave

step 1

Use toothpicks to dab food coloring on your marshmallows to decorate them.

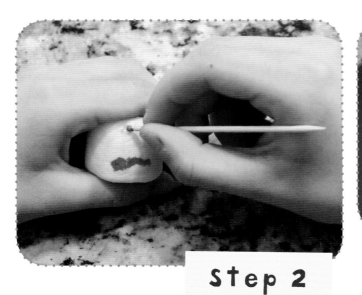

step 2

When done, put them on a plate that is safe to use in the microwave.

Step 3

Microwave them for 1 minute. Watch them grow through the window! Watch them deflate as you pull them out of the microwave.

HOW DOES IT WORK?

Marshmallows seem solid, but they have lots of air bubbles in them, along with sugar and water. When they heat up so quickly, the air bubbles expand, pushing against the stretchy walls of the molecule. The marshmallow expands.

Is a marshmallow a vegetable? Not quite. This is a marshmallow plant. Mixed with honey, the root of the plant was used medicinally to soothe sore throats. In the 1800s, the root began to be mixed with sugar, water, and egg whites to form candy. Over time, however, gelatin began to replace marshmallow root in the candy that bears the plant's name.

MINERALS AND CRYSTALS

Geologists study the materials that make up our Earth—rocks and minerals. You probably recognize the names of some of the most valuable minerals that can be made into gemstones. Amber, emerald, topaz, and diamond are all minerals. But there are thousands of minerals, some very obscure. Some are hard, while others are soft. Some are clear, while others are colorful. What do they have in common? They are all solid. They all occur in nature. They are not organic—that is, they are not made from living things. And each mineral has a fixed chemical makeup made up from the same combination of elements.

CRYSTALS

Many minerals have a crystalline structure. When you look at them through a microscope, their atoms or molecules are arranged in an orderly, repeating pattern.

The salt you use at the table is a mineral with a crystalline structure.

What does your pencil have in common with a diamond?

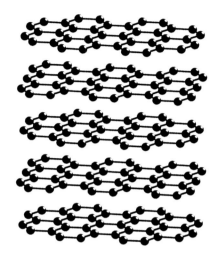

Both graphite and diamond are minerals made of a single element, carbon. But they have different crystalline structures.

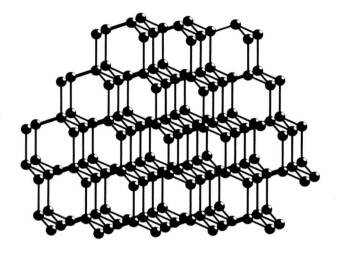

GRAPHITE

DIAMOND

TYPES OF MINERALS

Scientists divide minerals into groups based on their chemical makeups. Silicates like quartz and feldspar are the most common minerals, and make up most of the Earth's top layer, its crust. All silicates contain the elements oxygen and silicon.

Some other important groups of minerals include carbonates and oxides. Carbonates contain carbon and oxygen. Oxides contain oxygen and a metal.

Emerald and aquamarine are color variations of a silicate called beryl.

SALT AND PEPPER

Salt is a mineral, while pepper comes from a plant.
Use this trick to separate them if they get mixed up.

MATERIALS

- Salt
- Pepper
- Balloon

Step 1

Pour a small pile of salt and a small pile of pepper onto a flat surface.

Step 2

Mix the salt and pepper together.

step 3

Inflate a balloon and rub it against a sweater to generate static electricity. Hold the balloon above your pile. Slowly lower it closer to the pile until the pepper begins to react.

step 4

The pepper jumps up to the surface of the balloon! If you hold your balloon even closer, the salt will begin to jump up as well.

HOW DOES IT WORK?

Static electricity is the buildup of electric charge in an object. Protons carry a positive (+) charge, and electrons carry a negative (-) charge. Objects that have opposite charges will attract, or pull together. Objects with the same charge will repel, or push apart. When you rub the balloon on a sweater, it picks up extra electrons, giving the balloon a negative charge. This pushes the electrons away in the pile of salt and pepper, leaving a positive charge. The negatively-charged balloon attracts the positively-charged salt and pepper, causing them both to jump up. But since pepper is lighter, it jumps up more quickly.

If you don't have a balloon, you can charge a plastic fork or comb with static electricity in the same way and use that.

GROW A STALACTITE

In caves, stalactites form over years from mineral deposits. You can see the principles in action with this simple kitchen experiment.

MATERIALS

- Two jars or glasses
- A piece of yarn (about 1 foot long)
- Baking soda
- Water
- Paper clips
- Spoon
- Bowl
- Cardboard (optional)

Step 1

Spoon or pour baking soda into a jar of warm water. Stir until the water is cloudy and the baking soda begins to settle at the bottom of the jar instead of dissolving. Do the same with the other jar.

Step 2

Set up the jars with a bowl between them. It's best to do this on a surface that can be thrown out or easily wiped down, such as a piece of newspaper or cardboard. Because this experiment can take several days, it should also be somewhere out of the way.

Step 3

Step 4

Dip the ends of the yarn in each jar, so that they are resting in the water.

Secure the yarn to the jars with paper clips.

Step 5

Watch your stalactite grow over the next few days!

FOR FURTHER FUN

Try this experiment with sugar or salt, which also form crystals.

Caves form over thousands of years. Many caves are made of limestone. As water seeps into the cave, it carries acids that carve the limestone into strange and varied shapes, making features such as stalactites and stalagmites. Stalactites grow from the ceiling, while stalagmites grow from the ground.

CHEMICAL REACTIONS

In a chemical reaction, one set of substances is changed into another set of substances. The first set of substances, the **reactants**, are transformed into **products** when the bonds between atoms in the reactants are broken so that new molecules can be formed.

Rust is the result of a chemical reaction. Iron and oxygen are the reactants. They transform into the product iron oxide.

Fire is a chemical reaction.

FAST OR SLOW

Some chemical reactions happen very quickly. Others happen more slowly. You can speed up a chemical reaction by increasing energy. Energy in the form of heat, for example, can speed up the chemical reactions that occur when you are baking something. Sometimes another substance, called a **catalyst,** can be added to the chemical reaction to speed it up. An **inhibitor** slows a chemical reaction down.

Kimchi, yogurt, and many pickles are all created through a chemical process called fermentation. Yogurt, for example, is created when bacteria are added to milk. The bacteria changes lactose, a sugar in the milk, into lactic acid.

THE AMAZING DISAPPEARING EGGSHELL

What chemical reaction occurs when an egg is immersed in vinegar? Try it and see.

MATERIALS

- Mason jars or glasses
- Egg(s)
- Vinegar
- Food coloring (optional)

step 1

Fill a jar or jars with vinegar.

Step 2

For a cool effect, add food coloring.

Step 3

Add an egg to each jar or glass you use. Always wash your hands after handling raw eggs.

Step 4

Put the eggs in the refrigerator. After several hours, you will see them begin to float to the top of the jar. You will see bubbles begin to form as well.

Step 5

Leave the eggs in the refrigerator overnight.

What will you see when you draw them out?

THE EGGSHELL HAS DISAPPEARED!

Compared to a regular egg, the egg will also seem slightly larger.

WHERE DOES THE EGGSHELL GO?

Eggshell has a substance called calcium carbonate in it. The acid in vinegar breaks down the calcium carbonate. The bubbles are caused by the creation of carbon dioxide as it does so.

COLORFUL VEGGIES

Why do vegetables change colors as they are roasted?
Find out while you help prepare and eat dinner!

INGREDIENTS

- Vegetables
- Olive oil
- Seasonings such as salt, pepper, garlic powder

Step 1

Wash the vegetables. An adult should chop them up.

Step 2

Add olive oil to coat the vegetables. Add seasoning.

Step 3

Put the vegetables in a pan covered with foil.

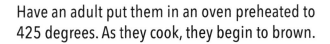

Step 4

Have an adult put them in an oven preheated to 425 degrees. As they cook, they begin to brown.

Step 5

After fifteen or twenty minutes, your veggies will be ready to eat!

WHY DO VEGGIES BROWN AS THEY BAKE?

Heat changes vegetables, both their color and their taste. A chemical reaction called caramelization occurs that affects the natural sugars in the vegetables, deepening their color to brown and altering their flavor.

PANCAKE CHEMISTRY

With an adult, make pancakes and see chemical reactions happen.

INGREDIENTS

- 1 ½ cups flour
- 3 ½ teaspons baking powder
- 1 egg
- 3 tablespoons melted butter
- 1 ¼ cups milk
- 1 tablespoon white sugar

Step 1

Mix all the ingredients in a measuring cup or bowl.

Step 2

Do you see bubbles form? That is a chemical reaction caused by the baking powder.

Step 3

An adult should pour the batter onto the griddle.

Step 4

Notice how bubbles form in the batter.

Step 5

An adult should flip the pancake over.

Step 6

Eat with syrup. *Why did the pancake turn brown?*

THE MAILLARD REACTION

When pancakes cook, they go through something called the Maillard reaction. Your ingredients contain both proteins, which have amino acids, and sugars. When heat is applied, the amino acids and the sugars go through a chemical reaction that produces the smell, the flavor, and the color of finished pancakes! The bubbles throughout the process are caused by the baking powder. It releases carbon dioxide.

SODA FOUNTAIN

Create a soda geyser with a chemical reaction between Mentos and Diet Coke.

MATERIALS

- Paper
- Tape
- Mentos
- 2 liter bottle of Diet Coke

Perform this experiment outdoors, using goggles or glasses. Keep your face away from the bottle.

Step 1

If you'd like, decorate the piece of paper.

Step 2

Roll the paper into a baton and tape it.

Step 3

Unscrew the lid of the soda bottle.

Step 4

Add a tube of Mentos to the tube of paper.

Step 5

Position the tube above the soda, keeping your finger on the end until you're ready to let them fall.

Step 6

Release the Mentos and step back!

ACIDS AND BASES

One way to classify a liquid is to ask whether it is an acid or a base. When you dissolve an acid in water, it releases a hydrogen ion—a positively charged hydrogen atom (H+). When you dissolve a base in water, it releases a hydroxide ion—a negatively charged molecule made from oxygen and hydrogen (OH-).

LITMUS PAPER

Lichens are organisms made from algae and fungi. The pigments in lichens have been used to make dye. A special kind of paper called litmus paper uses these dyes. Long before scientists knew about the chemistry behind acids and bases, they knew that some substances (bases) turned litmus paper blue and some substances (acids) turned it red.

pH SCALE

The 14-point pH scale is used to measure how basic or acidic a substance is when compared to water, which is neutral on the scale. Substances on either end of the scale that are strongly acidic or strongly basic (or alkaline) are dangerous to humans.

Have you ever had an upset stomach? Medicines like antacids work by neutralizing stomach acid.

Many acids taste sour to us. Citric acid gives grapefruit a sour flavor.

ACIDIC

0	battery	
1	stomach acid	
2	lemon	
3	soda	
4	tomato	
5	coffee	
6	milk	

NEUTRAL

7	water	
8	blood	
9	egg white	
10	stomach tablets	
11	ammonia solution	
12	soap	
13	bleach	

ALKALINE

| 14 | drain cleaner | |

PICKLES

Use the acid vinegar to transform cucumbers into pickles!

INGREDIENTS

An adult should do all the cutting in this experiment.

- 3-4 pickling cucumbers
- 1 ½ teaspoons coarse-grained kosher salt
- ¼ cup white distilled vinegar

- 1 clove garlic (optional)
- ¼ teaspoon dill seed (optional)
- ¼ teaspoon mustard seed (optional)

step 1

Have an adult cut the cucumbers into thin slices and add them to a one-pint Mason jar.

step 2

Add the vinegar to the jar.

step 3

Add 1 ½ teaspoons salt to the jar.

step 4

Add ¼ teaspoon dill seeds.

Step 5

Add ¼ teaspoon mustard seeds.

Step 6

Have an adult mince the garlic and add it to the jar. Seal the jar. Note how high the vinegar rises and how high the cucumbers are in the jar. Shake the jar to mix the ingredients.

Step 7

Put the jar in the fridge. Shake it at the one hour mark.

Step 8

Check again and shake the jar at the two hour mark. Note that the height of the liquid in the jar has gone up, as the salt pulls the water out of the cucumbers. Taste test a pickle.

Step 9

Over the next several days, see how the taste of the pickles changes. They will also change color over time. In this picture, you can see a cucumber before it is put in the brine, a pickle at one day, and a pickle at one week.

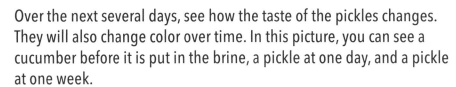

Fridge pickles last about two to three weeks. The salt and the vinegar are the key ingredients for changing cucumbers into pickles; the vinegar's acidity acts as a preservative. The other ingredients are optional and add flavor. You can leave out any you don't like, or try other ingredients like fresh dill, garlic powder, peppercorns, or coriander seeds.

Some pickles are made through the process of fermentation. In the process of fermentation, a chemical reaction occurs through the interaction of the food's sugars and bacteria.

RED CABBAGE CHEMISTRY

In this experiment, you'll make a pH indicator solution from red cabbage and use the solution to test whether substances are acids or bases.

Step 1

With an adult's help, chop the red cabbage into small pieces on a cutting board until you have about 2½ cups.

MATERIALS

- 2 ½ cups of red cabbage
- 3 clear glasses
- Sharp knife
- Cutting board
- Medium saucepan
- Strainer
- Large measuring cup
- ¼ cup vinegar
- 1 teaspoon baking soda
- Spoon
- Water

Step 2

Place cut up cabbage in a medium saucepan and cover with water. Bring to a boil and then turn off heat. Let cabbage steep, stirring occasionally, for about 25 minutes or until room temperature.

Step 3

Pour the cabbage mixture through a strainer and into a large measuring cup. This dark purple liquid is the indicator solution you will use.

Step 4

Prepare 3 glasses with your test samples. In the first glass, pour about ¼ cup of vinegar. In the second glass, pour about ¼ cup of plain water. This is neutral, or the control. In the third glass, mix a teaspoon or so of baking soda into about ¼ cup water. Stir until dissolved.

Step 5

Pour some of your cabbage indicator solution into the first glass of vinegar. Stir with a spoon and notice the color change. *What color does the liquid become?*

Step 6

Pour some of your cabbage indicator solution into the second glass of plain water and stir. *Does the color of the liquid change, or does it stay the same purple color as the original indicator solution?*

Step 7

Pour some of your cabbage indicator solution into the third glass of baking soda. Stir with a spoon and watch the color change. *What color does the liquid become? What would happen if you added more baking soda to the glass?*

HOW DOES IT WORK?

Red cabbage contains a pigment called anthocyanin that changes color when it is mixed with an acid or a base. The pigment turns reddish-pink in acidic environments and bluish-green in alkaline (basic) environments. Your first glass turned reddish-pink because vinegar is an acid. Your second glass of plain water didn't change color because water is neutral. Your third glass turned blue because baking soda is a base.

SOAPY SHAKE

Baking soda is a base. Lemon is an acid. See how they react with each other! This can overflow the glass, so make sure you're in an area that can be cleaned easily.

MATERIALS

- Tall glass
- Spoonful of baking soda
- A few squirts of dishwashing detergent
- Lemon juice (½ cup to a cup)
- Food coloring (optional)

Step 1

Drop a few spoonfuls of baking soda into the glass.

Step 2

Squirt some dishwashing detergent on top of the baking soda.

Step 3

Step 4

If desired, add a few drops of food coloring. We added red food coloring to ours.

Begin pouring lemon juice into your glass. Stir. As the baking soda reacts to the lemon, a soapy, bubbly concoction will rise slowly in the glass.

If needed, add more baking soda or more lemon juice.

HOW DOES IT WORK?

Baking soda is a base. Lemon juice is an acid. When they mix, it creates bubbles of carbon dioxide. The gas bubbles interact with the dishwashing detergent, and you end up with a soapy shake—you can't drink it, but you could clean dishes with it!

INFLATE A BALLOON

Can you inflate a balloon without blowing into it or using a pump? You can if you combine a liquid and a solid to make a gas.

Step 1

Stretch out the balloon before you begin by inflating it fully and then deflating it. This will allow the balloon to more easily expand during the experiment.

MATERIALS

- Balloon
- Empty water bottle
- 2 teaspoons baking soda
- ⅓ cup vinegar
- Funnel

Step 2

Use a funnel to add 2 teaspoons of baking soda to the deflated balloon.

Step 3

Use a small binder clip to close the upper neck of the balloon, leaving enough room at the end to stretch over the bottle's neck.

Step 4

Pour ⅓ cup of vinegar into the empty bottle.

Step 5

Keeping the baking soda in the body of the balloon, carefully stretch the neck of the balloon over the neck of the bottle.

Step 6

Remove the binder clip. Lift the balloon up and allow the baking soda to fall into the vinegar. *What do you observe? How long does it take the balloon to fully inflate? How long does the balloon remain inflated?*

HOW DOES IT WORK?

The balloon inflates because of a chemical reaction between the baking soda (a base) and vinegar (an acid). When the baking soda and vinegar mix, a gas called carbon dioxide, or CO_2, is created. The gas in the bottle has nowhere to go but into the balloon, so the balloon inflates. Similarly, we exhale carbon dioxide when we blow up balloons.

ERUPTING VOLCANO

Make a model volcano and then cause an eruption with a chemical reaction.

MATERIALS

- Air-dry clay
- Disposable cup
- Small container
- Paper plate
- Tape
- Cardboard
- Scissors
- Wax paper
- Small dish of water
- Paint
- Measuring cup
- ¼ cup vinegar
- 1 teaspoon baking soda
- 1 teaspoon dishwashing liquid
- Few drops of water
- Red food coloring

Step 1

Tape a small container onto the top of an upside-down disposable cup to form the crater. We are using a 3¼-ounce condiment container on top of a 9-ounce cup.

Step 2

Cut strips of cardboard about 5 inches (12.7 cm) long and 1¾ inches (4.5 cm) wide. Cereal boxes work great. Tape the cardboard strips to the sides of the crater container at the top.

Step 3

Tape the bottom of the cardboard strips to the paper plate.

Step 4

Place wax paper down on your work surface. Scoop out some air-dry clay.

Step 5

Form clay into thin strips by flattening it between fingers or by pressing clay down onto the wax paper and spreading it out.

Step 6

Place clay strips onto the sides of the volcano structure. Dip fingertips in small dish of water and mold volcano pieces together. Use smaller pieces of clay to fill in gaps.

Step 7

Allow clay to dry completely on paper plate. This usually takes 2–3 days. It's okay if it's lumpy or cracked–so are real volcanoes!

Step 8

Paint and decorate volcano as desired. We used 2 coats of brown spray paint. Once paint is dry, you are ready for the eruption.

Step 9

Mix ¼ cup vinegar, about 1 teaspoon of dishwashing liquid, a few drops of water, and a few drops of red food coloring in a measuring cup.

Step 10

Add 1 teaspoon baking soda to the crater container at the top of your volcano. The paper plate will help keep your eruption mess to a minimum, but it's smart to place the plate on an easily cleaned surface.

Step 11

Quickly pour the vinegar mixture into the crater container with baking soda and watch your volcano erupt!

HOW DOES IT WORK?

The baking soda reacts with the vinegar in the mixture and produces carbon dioxide (CO_2) gas. The gas releases bubbles through the dishwashing liquid and food coloring, creating the bubbly, orange lava that erupts from your volcano.

HEAT AND COLD

Heat is a form of energy, also called thermal energy. When a substance is hot, the atoms and molecules inside it are moving quickly. When a substance is cold, the atoms and molecules inside it are moving slowly.

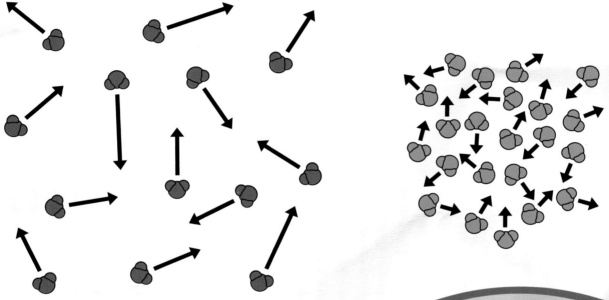

FROM HOT TO COLD

When you put something hot near something cold, the heat moves from the hotter object to the colder object until equilibrium is reached. When heat moves directly from one object to another, it is called conduction. Have you ever touched something metal, like a doorknob, when it is hot outside? You probably pulled your hand away quickly, because it was too hot! Some materials, like metals, conduct heat very well.

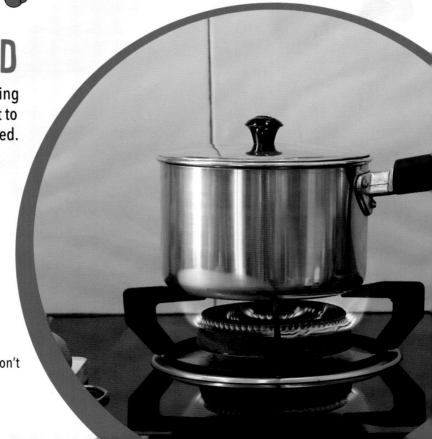

Many pots are made of metal to conduct heat quickly from the stove to the food inside the pan. But the handle is usually made of or coated with a material that inhibits the transfer of heat, so you don't burn your hand.

KEEPING COLD

If you've ever eaten a popsicle quickly on a hot day to keep it from melting, you know that keeping something cool can be a challenge. What did people do to store food before they had a refrigerator or freezer? Underground caves and cellars helped people keep food cool so it would last longer.

In the 1800s and early 1900s, many people had iceboxes. Companies collected ice in the winter and stored it. An iceman would then bring a daily shipment of ice to his customers for use in their icebox.

This picture from 1923 shows an iceman making his deliveries.

FISHING FOR ICE

Use a piece of yarn and a little bit of salt to "fish" for ice cubes.

MATERIALS

- Glass of water
- Ice cubes
- Yarn
- Salt
- Stopwatch or timer on a phone

Step 1

Fill a glass with cold water and ice.

Step 2

Rest the yarn on top of the ice. The yarn does not stick to the ice.

Step 3

Pour a bit of salt on top of the ice cubes and yarn.

Step 4

Wait at least 30 seconds.

Step 5

Gently tug on the yarn. This time, the ice sticks to the yarn.

Step 6

How many ice cubes can you pick up?

HOW DOES IT WORK?

Adding salt to ice changes its freezing point, allowing it to melt and refreeze around the yarn. In areas that get snowfall, people put salt and other materials on the roads and on their driveways to melt the ice and snow and make it safe to drive.

ICE CREAM

You can make your own ice cream.

MATERIALS

- Bowl of ice
- 1 cup of water
- Salt
- Thermometer
- 1 gallon zipper bag
- Smaller zipper bag
- 1 teaspoon vanilla
- ½ cup of sugar

step 1

Measure the temperature of the ice bowl.

Step 2

Add salt to the bowl of ice.

Step 3

It's colder. Why? The salt lowers the freezing point of the ice.

Step 4

Add milk to the smaller bag.

Step 5

Add the sugar.

Step 6

Add the vanilla.

Step 7

Zip up the bag.

Step 8

Add salty ice from the bowl to the larger bag and place the smaller bag inside it.

Step 9

Zip it up.

Step 10

Shake and squeeze the bags for 5 to 10 minutes. This prevents the ice crystals forming inside the ice cream from getting too large and keeps your ice cream smooth and creamy.

Step 11

Pull out the smaller bag.

Step 12

You have ice cream!

BAKED...ICE CREAM?

Can a dessert be hot and cold at once? Baked Alaska can.

MATERIALS

- Ice cream
- Plastic wrap
- Glass bowls
- Four eggs
- 2 cups of sugar
- ½ teaspoon cream of tartar
- Chocolate cake
- Ovenproof plate

Step 1

Line a bowl with plastic wrap.

Step 2

Put ice cream in the bowl, smashing it down flat. Put the bowl in the freezer for an hour.

Step 3

Take the ice cream out of the bowl and place it upside down on the cake. The plate you use needs to be ovenproof.

Step 4

Separate the yolks of the eggs from the whites. Discard the yolks. Always wash your hands when handling raw eggs.

Step 5

Beat the egg whites in a mixing bowl until they are frothy. You are making the meringue that goes on top.

Step 6

Add the cream of tartar and whisk the egg whites again.

Step 7

Add the sugar.

Step 8

Continue to beat the mixture until it is shiny and can form stiff peaks.

Step 9

Use a spatula to quickly and carefully coat the ice cream and cake with the meringue.

Step 10

Have an adult pop the Baked Alaska into an oven preheated to 450 degrees for three minutes.

Step 11

Using oven mitts, the adult should take the Baked Alaska out of the oven. Let it cool for a minute, then slice into it. Amazingly, the ice cream has not melted!

WHY DOESN'T THE ICE CREAM MELT?

The egg whites contain a protein called albumin. When you beat the egg whites, the albumin molecules rearrange in a way that traps lots of tiny air bubbles. The air bubbles trap the heat, baking the surface of the dessert while leaving the ice cream inside intact.

SOLAR OVEN PIZZA BOX

Foil, dark construction paper, and plastic wrap all help intensify heat energy from the Sun in order to melt food. Try this project on a hot, sunny day.

MATERIALS

- Clean pizza box
- Aluminum foil
- Plastic wrap
- Black construction paper
- Ruler
- Tape
- Scissors
- Marshmallows
- Pencils or pen

step 1

Draw three sides of a square on the top of your pizza box.

step 2

Cut along the lines to make a second lid that can be raised and lowered.

Step 3

Wrap the flap with foil. Use tape if necessary.

Step 4

Add foil to the bottom of the box.

Step 5

Add black paper to the bottom of the box.

Step 6

Add food. Do not use food that can spoil in heat.

Step 7

Wrap the box in plastic wrap and set it in a sunny spot. Prop open the foil lid with a pencil.

Step 8

The food inside will gradually melt! The plastic wrap traps the heat inside.

POLYMERS AND PLASTICS

A polymer is a special kind of molecule–a very large one made up of chains of smaller molecules that are called monomers. "Poly" is just a prefix meaning "many," while "mono" means one.

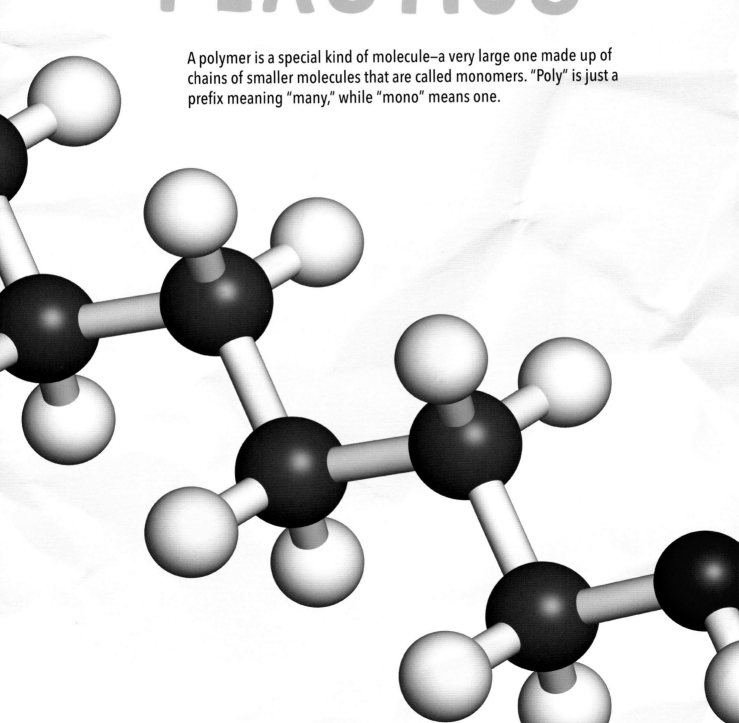

NATURAL POLYMERS

Wool and silk are polymers. The cellulose found in trees and paper is a polymer, too. Proteins are polymers made up of monomers called amino acids.

SYNTHETIC POLYMERS

Inventors began creating synthetic polymers that mimicked natural ones. Sometimes they adapted natural polymers. For example, rubber is a natural polymer, but people began to make modifications to make it more useful. Eventually people began to create fully synthetic polymers such as nylon.

PLASTICS

Plastics are synthetic polymers. They're named for their plasticity—meaning they can be shaped easily. The first plastic, Bakelite, was invented in 1907. Today plastics are everywhere. One worry that people have is that there are too many plastics! They do not degrade easily. People are now working on biodegradable plastics and recyclable plastics.

LEAKPROOF BAG

What do you think will happen when a plastic bag full of water is punctured by pencils?

MATERIALS

- Clear zippered plastic bag
- Pitcher of water
- Sharpened pencils

Step 1

Fill the plastic bag most of the way with water. It helps to have someone else hold open the bag for you. Seal the top of the bag tightly so no water or air escapes.

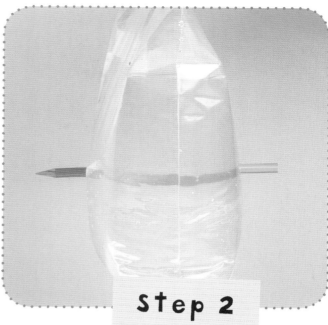

Step 2

Hold the bag at the top with one hand. Push the first pencil, sharpened end first, through one side of the bag and partway out the other side. *Did any water leak out?*

Make sure your pencils are sharpened!

Step 3

Repeat step 2 with the other pencils. *Did any water leak?* When you're done, remove the pencils over a sink or outside.

HOW DOES IT WORK?

The plastic bag is made out of low-density polyethylene, a strong but flexible material. It contains long chains of molecules called polymers. The tip of the pencil slips between the chains without breaking them. The chains' flexible property helps form a temporary seal around the pencil. This allows the pencil to pierce the bag without leaking any water.

MILK PLASTIC

You can make plastic toys out of milk, which contains a protein polymer called casein.

MATERIALS

- Small pot
- Stove
- 2 cups of milk
- 8 teaspoons of vinegar
- Strainer
- Cookie cutters
- Sunny day
- Paint (optional)

Step 1

Pour the milk in a pot.

Step 2

Have an adult heat the milk over medium heat, stirring constantly.

Step 3

Add the vinegar and stir it in.

step 4

Keep stirring for 1 minute. Curds will begin to form.

Step 5

Strain out the liquids, leaving the curds.

step 6

Squish out the excess liquid with a spoon.

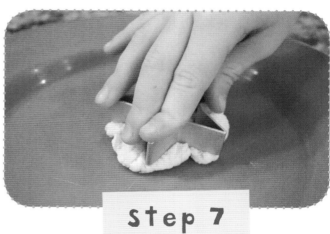

Step 7

Cut the curds into shapes.

Step 8

Set the curds outside to dry.

Step 9

Decorate with paint!

MILK SWIRL

A drop of detergent creates a beautiful image.

MATERIALS

- A cup of whole milk
- Shallow dish or bowl
- Food coloring
- Dish detergent

Step 1

Pour the milk into the dish, covering the bottom.

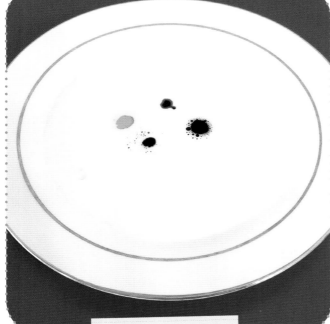

Step 2

Add 4–6 drops of different colors of food coloring near the center of the dish.

Step 3

Add a drop of dishwashing detergent to the center of the dish.

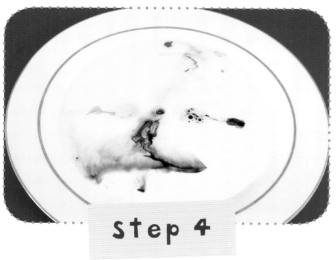

step 4

The food coloring will begin to react immediately!

step 5

Watch the milk swirl! *How does the pattern change over time?*

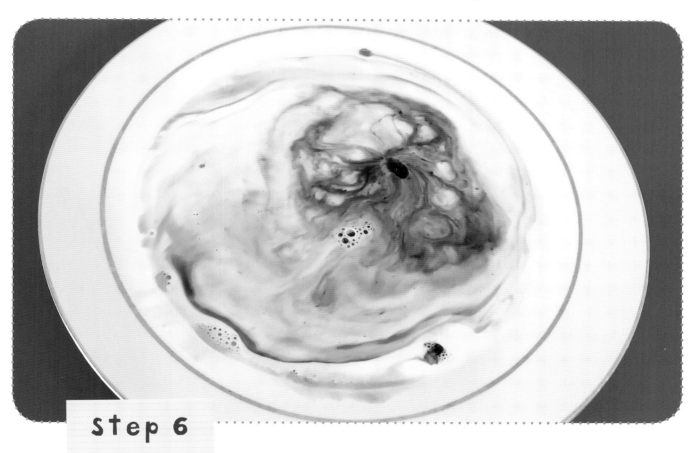

step 6

Tilt the dish a bit to create a different pattern.

HOW DOES IT WORK?

The detergent breaks up the fat molecules in the milk, creating a colorful reaction. Whole milk works best for this as it has the highest fat content.

BATTERIES

Batteries are a way to store power. When a battery is used, it transforms chemical energy into electrical energy. Batteries have two electrodes, one positive and one negative, with chemicals (electrolytes) in between. Current flows from one electrode to the other.

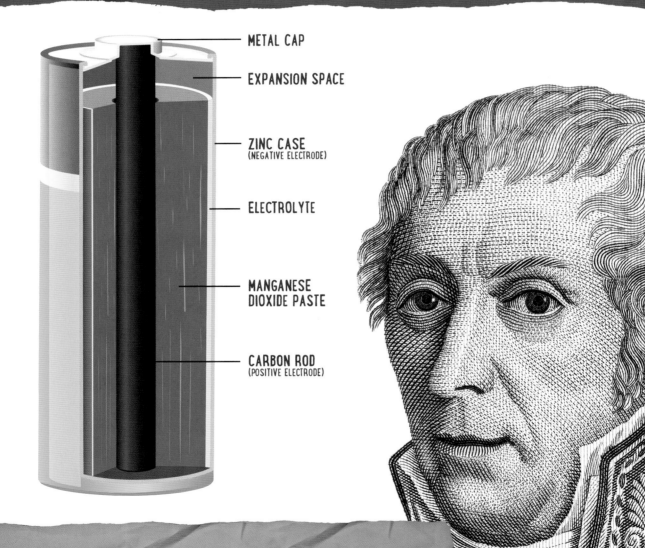

METAL CAP

EXPANSION SPACE

ZINC CASE
(NEGATIVE ELECTRODE)

ELECTROLYTE

MANGANESE
DIOXIDE PASTE

CARBON ROD
(POSITIVE ELECTRODE)

Alessandro Volta, an Italian physicist, created the first electrochemical battery in 1880. He was able to produce current from a stack of zinc and copper plates.

Alkaline batteries typically contain zinc and manganese dioxide. The reaction between the two produces the energy.

Have you ever opened a dead flashlight or remote control to replace the alkaline batteries, only to find that the battery is not just dead but corroded? The chemical reactions that take place in the battery produce its energy. But over time, those chemical reactions can also produce hydrogen gas, creating pressure that causes a leak of an electrolyte called potassium hydroxide. When potassium hydroxide interacts with air, it creates a white powdery substance called potassium carbonate. An acid such as vinegar can be used to clean it off the device.

Li-ion Battery
3.7V 3500 mA/h

Smartphones use rechargeable lithium-ion batteries.

LEMON BATTERY

Make a battery using lemons. Then find out if your lemon battery can make an electric current flow around a circuit with enough energy to illuminate a small lamp called a light emitting diode (LED).

MATERIALS

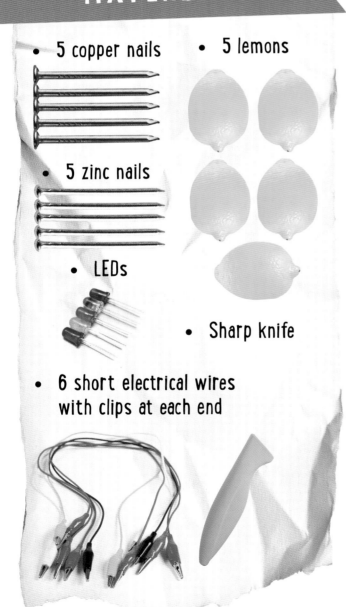

- 5 copper nails
- 5 lemons
- 5 zinc nails
- LEDs
- Sharp knife
- 6 short electrical wires with clips at each end

Step 1

Begin by rolling the lemons on a table to get them softer and juicier. With an adult's help, use a sharp knife to cut two slits in each lemon. The slits should be about 1¼ inches (3 cm) apart and about ½ inch (1¼ cm) deep.

Step 2

For each lemon, insert a galvanized (zinc-covered) nail into one slit and a copper nail into the other. Arrange the lemons in a circle with the zinc nails next to the copper nails in the adjacent lemons.

Step 3

Squeeze open the clip on one side of an electrical wire and fasten it onto a copper nail. Fasten the clip on the other side onto a zinc nail in the next lemon.

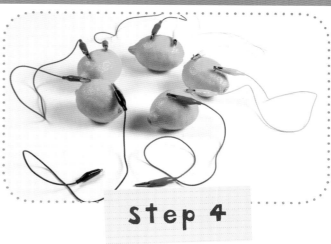

Step 4

Connect all of the lemons—copper nail to zinc nail—as in step 3, except for the first and last lemons. Instead, fasten a clip onto the first lemon's zinc nail and leave the other clip unconnected. Fasten a clip onto the last lemon's copper nail and leave the other clip unconnected.

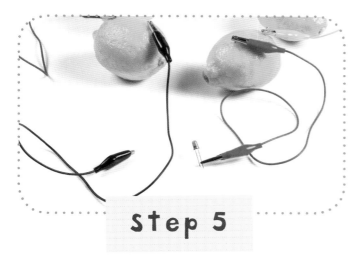

Step 5

Each LED has two legs that are slightly different lengths. With the free end of the wire that is attached to the copper nail, fasten the clip onto the slightly longer leg of the LED.

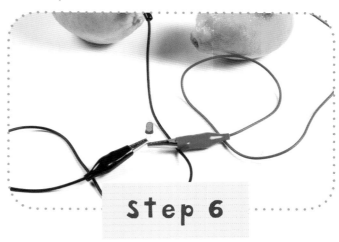

Step 6

With the free end of the wire attached to the zinc nail, fasten the clip onto the shorter leg of the LED. This completes the circuit to make the LED light up. The LED is very faint, so you might want to dim other lights to see it.

HOW DOES IT WORK?

The electric current that lights your LED is actually caused by countless tiny particles called electrons moving around the circuit. Electrons are present inside every atom. As the zinc dissolves in the lemon juice, two electrons are released from each atom of zinc (from the zinc-covered nail). All electrons are negatively charged, and they push apart as they move inside the wire. When they reach the copper nail, they take part in another chemical reaction, allowing electrons to continue flowing around the circuit.

THE COLOR WHEEL

PRIMARY COLORS

The primary colors are red, yellow, and blue. When we say primary colors, what we mean is that these three colors are the source of all other colors. Primary colors cannot be mixed or created from other colors. What do you think is the most popular color in the world? The answer is blue.

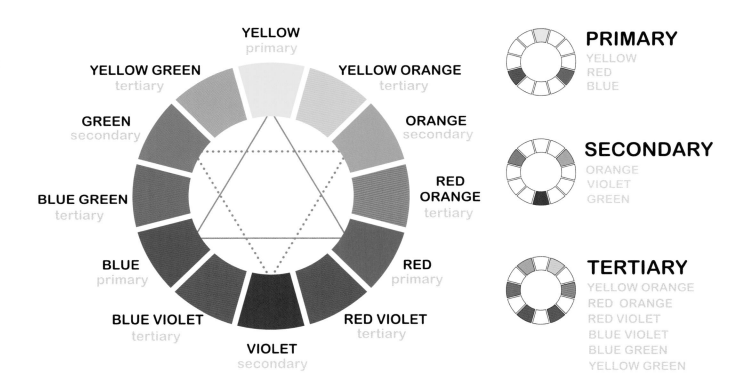

SECONDARY COLORS

The secondary colors are orange, green, and purple. Secondary colors are made by mixing two of the primary colors. The way to make each of these colors specifically is: blue and yellow make green, yellow and red make orange, and red and blue make purple. What's neat is that the amount of each color you use when mixing the primary colors produces a different shade of the secondary color. Amounts matter! If you add more red than yellow to a red-yellow mix, you get a reddish-orange, and if you add more yellow than red, you get a yellowish-orange.

COMPLEMENTARY COLORS

Complementary colors are any two colors that are directly opposite each other on the color wheel, for example, red and green. For each of the three secondary colors, their complementary color is the one primary color that was not used to create it. So, for orange, it's blue and for purple, it's yellow. If you want to make a color really stick out, try placing complementary colors next to each other. This visually intensifies both colors!

Florists often use flowers of complementary colors as they create a bouquet.

When white light enters a prism, it breaks into its separate colors. Basically, the glass causes the light to bend. Since each color travels at a different speed, it bends a different amount, producing a rainbow effect.

PRIMARY AND SECONDARY COLORS

Let's say you want your food to be orange, green, and purple, but you only have red, yellow, and blue food coloring. No problem!

MATERIALS

- Three glasses
- Red, yellow, and blue food coloring
- Water

step 1

Fill three glasses with water.

step 2

step 3

Add a few drops of red food coloring to the first glass.   Add a few drops of yellow food coloring.

Step 4

Stir the food coloring into the water. Red and yellow make orange!

Step 5

Add a few drops of yellow food coloring to the second glass.

Step 6

Add a few drops of blue food coloring to the second glass.

Step 7

Stir the food coloring into the water. Yellow and blue make green!

Step 8

Add a few drops of red food coloring to the last glass.

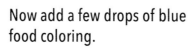

Step 9

Now add a few drops of blue food coloring.

Step 10

Red and blue make purple!

COLORFUL CANDY

Create a pretty pattern with candy and water!

MATERIALS

- Small, shallow dish
- Hard-shelled candy such as M&Ms
- Water

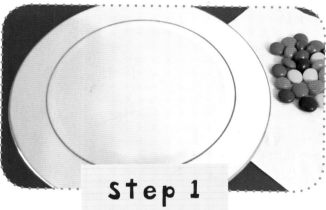

Step 1

Pour water into the dish.

Step 2

Line the dish with candy.

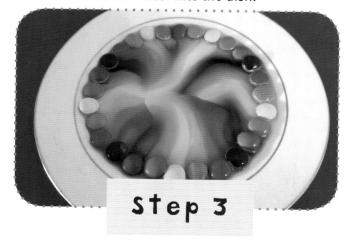

Step 3

The water leaches out the dye in the candy shell.

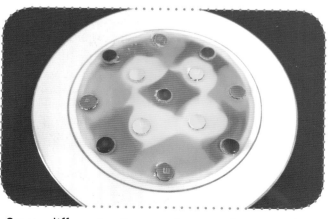

Create different patterns using your favorite colors!